An Easy-To-Follow Checklist To
Monetizing Your Instagram Account
and Turn it Into a Sales Machine

Instagram   Monet-

ization Checklist

Instagram Monetization Checklist

EXCLUSIVE REPORT

"Instagram Monetization Checklist"

Instagram Monetization Checklist

DISCLAIMER

This e-book has been written for information purposes only. Every effort has been made to make this ebook as complete and accurate as possible. However, there may be mistakes in typography or content. Also, this e-book provides information only up to the publishing date. Therefore, this ebook should be used as a guide - not as the ultimate source.

The purpose of this ebook is to educate. The author and the publisher do not warrant that the information contained in this e-book is fully complete and shall not be responsible for any errors or omissions. The author and publisher shall have neither liability nor responsibility to any person or entity with respect to any loss or damage caused or alleged to be caused directly or indirectly by this ebook.

Instagram Monetization Checklist

INSTAGRAM MONETIZATION CHECKLIST

Each and every single month, more than 1 billion people log into Instagram, interact with content, and post content to the platform.

Far and away one of the most frequently visited and often utilized social media platforms, even more so than Facebook, Instagram has become the "go to" platform for serious business owners, advertisers, and marketers that are looking to build their business online.

And even though Instagram is 100% free to get started with – and you can have a brand-new Instagram account up and running in less than five minutes.

The truth of the matter is the overwhelming majority of business owners, advertisers, and marketers out there aren't using Instagram the right way to build their business or create the kind of financial future they have always dreamed of.

Honestly, the majority of the Instagram market is little more than "traditional marketing" applied to the digital world – and that just isn't going to cut the mustard any longer.

No, if you are going to knock your Instagram marketing right out of the park and really turn it into a powerful channel for marketing you have to know exactly what you're doing.

On top of that, because you're going up against already stiff and established competition, you also have to take advantage of as many shortcuts checklists as possible to get you to the top as fast as you can.

Here are some critical tips and tricks in this quick checklist that will help you do exactly that.

LET'S DIVE RIGHT IN!

Instagram Mon-
etization Checklist

START AT THE START – GET YOUR INSTAGRAM STRATEGY DOWN FIRST

Most folks run their marketing right off the rails at the start, never even realizing that their entire Instagram marketing and was built on a foundation of sand and not concrete.

Most people just kind of throw different marketing approaches at the wall of Instagram and hope that something sticks, rather than taking a real systematic and focused approach to creating marketing that actually has an opportunity of working.

BUT NOT YOU.

No, since you are reading this quick checklist and following along with all of the tips and tricks we were able to share, you are going to have an almost unfair advantage over the competition to create truly effective marketing that actually works.

You're going to be able to start at the start (where you need to create that solid foundation) and build from there.

IDENTIFY YOUR PERFECT PROSPECT

The very first thing you have to do (even before you create a new Instagram account) is come up with a crystal clear image of who your perfect prospect is.

You have to know what they are most interested in getting out of you, what they are most interested in seeing and interacting with on Instagram, and the "hot buttons" that compel them to go from engaged Instagram follower to paying customer as quickly as humanly possible.

Once you have this crystal clear image of who this perfect customer is you're going to want to craft each and every single piece of Instagram content you create (as well as every other piece of marketing you manufacture) for them and them alone.

Instagram Mon-
etization Checklist

A lot of people make the mistake of trying to be everything to everyone with their Instagram marketing, missing the mark completely and getting zero followers instead of laser targeting in on their specific niche while ignoring the overwhelming majority of people that wouldn't have become customers anyway.

STEAL GREAT IDEAS FROM YOUR COMPETITORS

After really firmly establishing that image of your perfect prospect it's time to go and look at the top 15 or 20 Instagram accounts in your industry, really trying to come up with an idea of what they are doing so effectively in your market to already.

> *There is absolutely no reason whatsoever to try and reinvent the wheel when it comes to online marketing, especially when your competitors (your successful competitors, anyway) will not have only blazed that trail for you to follow but will have left very easy to understand and copy clues for you as well.*

Some people get a little bit squeamish about "stealing" content ideas from competitors, but you are going to want to get past that as soon as humanly possible.

We aren't in any way suggesting that you actually rip off physical pieces of content and pass them off as your own, but if you are in an outdoor equipment niche in your best competitors are posting in sunup and sundown images of camp life you had better believe you are doing a lot of the exact same thing or you are going to be missing your mark with your ideal prospects and losing ground to these competitors for no reason whatsoever.

This will help you speed up your content marketing on Instagram significantly, but it will also help you slip right into the top tier of Instagram accounts in your industry when you're publishing the same content as the "big dogs" are.

CREATE A CONTENT MARKETING CALENDAR

THE CONTENT
MARKETING
CALENDAR IS THE
NUMBER ONE
DIFFERENTIATOR
BETWEEN AMATEUR
HOUR MARKETERS
ON INSTAGRAM AND
SERIOUS AND SAVVY
SOCIAL MEDIA

Instagram Mon-
etization Checklist

marketers, and you're definitely going to want to find yourself in the latter group.

Major companies all over the world have spent a tremendous amount of time, energy, and effort really trying to streamline and systemize as much of their customer acquisition process as possible.

And while these major multinational companies have budgets far bigger than anything any of us could ever muster, the one weapon that we can copy and use just effectively as they are is the content calendar.

> *Setting up your marketing six months (or even better, one year) in advance with a plan for every single piece of content you are going to release a very specific day and as part of a very specific marketing campaign gives you an almost unfair advantage over the rest of your competition.*

By setting out understanding that you are going to have to create content for a three times a week release you're not only able to create those posts in advance and get them ready for "prime time", you're also able to find just the right piece of content to publish at a particular point in time to dovetail in with all of the other marketing approaches you are utilizing.

With a content marketing calendar, you can be working on a Valentine's Day campaign, for example in the middle of June, coming up with content that will be released on Instagram that goes hand-in-hand with the Valentine's Day campaign you have been running from the end of January right up until the middle of February the coming year.

On top of that, you can really start to automate your Instagram marketing when you take this kind of approach.

Because you have all of your content created and ready to go, you can then script programs or outsource the actual publishing work to someone else – freeing up your time so that you can focus on other high leverage business activities without having to worry about how you're going to cobble together an advertising approach that day.

THIS IS GAME CHANGING STUFF, AND YOU HAVE TO BE 100% CERTAIN THAT YOU ARE DOING

EVERYTHING in your power to systemize, automate, and delegate as much of your Instagram marketing as possible.

Instagram Monetization Checklist

This checklist will go a long way towards helping you do exactly that, but the bulk of the work is going to come from creating content focused on your perfect prospect, content proven to work by your competitors, and content that is released on a regular and systemized basis according to your content calendar.

GROWTH, GROWTH, GROWTH – GROW AS BIG AND AS FAST AS YOU CAN

The next stage after laying your foundation and Instagram marketing is focusing entirely on growing your following just as quickly as humanly possible.

Instagram does a lot of the heavy lifting for you, helping to recommend your Instagram account to other people automatically and even actively promoting your account through Instagram posts of the day, hashtags, and the like, but you really want to take ownership of your Instagram marketing right out of the gate to grow your account as large as you're able to as fast as you're able to.

After all, the greatest content in the world, matched perfectly to your ideal customers, isn't going to be worth ANYTHING unless you are getting eyeballs and actively engaging people that have chosen to follow your Instagram account.

Without followers, all of your efforts are wasted completely – so you have to build that following up from the ground with lightning like speed.

HERE ARE SOME QUICK TIPS TO HELP YOU DO EXACTLY THAT!

PIGGYBACK OFF OF INSTAGRAM INFLUENCERS

Instagram influencers – the most frequently followed, engaged with, and active accounts in your market or industry – have the ability to lift any account that they regularly interact with, as well as any account that regularly interacts with them.

Instagram Monetization Checklist

You have to do everything in your power to either capture the attention of these Instagram influencers in your industry or your market so that they start to actively promote the content that you provide (and we will show you one way to do that in just a second) OR you have to try and "steal their thunder" as much as possible by mentioning them in your own content so much so that their followers start to pay attention to you as well.

> *Instagram marketing is quickly becoming an arms race of sorts, with major accounts releasing new posts on an hourly basis as opposed to a daily or even weekly update.*

Major accounts – we're talking about accounts with hundreds of thousands or even millions of followers – need to have a lot of activity to keep up with their hungry followers, and that means that they need a tremendous amount of original content that they have the chance to share.

That's where you as a "smaller operator" come into play!

Because you don't have to feed the same kind of beast (yet), you can actually afford to not only create content for your own Instagram account but content for these major Instagram account influencers as well.

By creating content that you then give to these influencers to share with their followers 100% free of charge (though with attribution and tags going back to your account), you are able to do them a favor while also serving your own needs.

These kinds of accounts are super happy to enter into these kinds of agreements.

They get a lot of free, high-quality content that they don't have to work hard to create, they keep their followers happy, and they get to partner with new up and comers in the same industry.

You'll also benefit from the extra exposure you get from these influencing Instagram accounts – and before you know it you will have floods in floods of followers diving headfirst into your account, turning you into an influencer as well!

CONTESTS WORKED WONDERS AS WELL

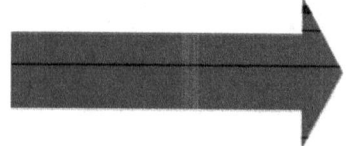

Instagram Monetization Checklist

Another great approach to growing your account quickly is to run regular contests where you actually give away high-quality items or services on your Instagram account in exchange for increased follower numbers.

This is a proven, tried and true, and amazingly effective marketing tactic and technique that has been in use long before Instagram was even thought of.

The only thing you have to do is fulfill your end of the deal – actually giving away whatever products or services you have promised to – and they cost you a little bit upfront, but when you actively monetize your Instagram account, you'll find that the return on investment is well worth it.

The bigger the item, the more exciting the service, and the more valuable the giveaway, the more action you are going to get and the more followers you are going to accumulate.

If you are in the golf niche, for example, giving away a sleeve of balls is barely going to move the needle. Giving away a trip to Pebble Beach, however, is going to have you swimming in more followers than you will know what to do with.

Sure, that trip to Pebble Beach is going to cost a lot more than a sleeve of balls, but as mentioned above the return on investment is going to be well worth it.

Instead of picking up a handful of followers for $12 you might pick up 10,000 new followers or more for $2000. The trade-off should be obvious.

CREATE MULTIPLE CHANNELS OF MONETIZATION WITH INSTAGRAM

At the end of the day, new followers aren't cold hard cash in the bank unless you actually begin to monetize your followers and your account on Instagram.

The easiest way to monetize your Instagram account is to simply use your account and your Instagram content as an entry-level to your marketing funnel.

Instagram Monetization Checklist

You'll be able to push visitors and followers to your account deeper and deeper into your marketing materials, converting at least some of them into paying customers – and that's got a pretty reasonable ROI.

Of course, there are other ways to monetize your Instagram account – and even if you do decide to sell your own products and services, you'll want to pursue some of these avenues to maximize your leverage on social media and create multiple income streams.

For starters, you can seek out other businesses in your industry – competitors or those offering complementary services – and offer to provide them with "sponsored content".

You basically become an affiliate for their company and any of the sales you drive through your Instagram account pay you get paid a commission.

This is how a lot of "Instagram models" make their money online, posting pictures of themselves and workout gear or using workout supplements provided by other companies and getting a cut of the affiliate sales they drive.

These people are making a steady income off of this kind of affiliate marketing alone, so it's definitely worth investigating.

There are plenty of ways to monetize Instagram, and hopefully, this quick checklist has shined a little bit of extra light on the subject for you going forward!

ARE YOU CUSTOM TAILORING YOUR PRODUCTS TO MATCH YOUR FOLLOWERS?

If you are interested in maximizing profit and turnover, then custom tailoring your product is an excellent way of going about it. There are several reasons as to why this is vital for your business. Below are five reasons why you should;

1.   Attention to Detail Pays Off

Here, the focus is in ways that will make your product stand out from the others. Do not only stand out for a classy logo and brand but also show you are caring enough for your product. This will consequently push you to design everything about your product to the last detail which clients will be able to see and make them want to buy.

2.   Understand Your Clients and Their Trends

When you start tailoring your product, it means you are understanding your customers' needs and wants. If you carry out a research about what your clients want and match it to your product line, then your message becomes very powerful. Producing products in line with customers' needs and preference will not only save you money but will also help your clients notice how much you care and socially responsible you are.

3. Customization Helps a Product Stand Out

Tailoring your products has very many advantages and does help one distinguish his/her products and stand out from competition. If your products appear to have taken some time to plan before hitting the market then what you are offering is likely to hold a strong foot in the market keeping your business going for years to come.

4. Prevent Bogusness

To effectively sell your product, allow clients to feel and come to a conclusion on their own instead of laying it out for them. Rather than reciting a long list of benefits and features, custom tailoring shows your service or product in action consequently making your product interesting to want to have a second look.

5. Comprehensive Packaging Services

By tailoring your products, one also stands at an advantage of gaining numerous offers from other related service providers. For instance, one can sign a managed inventory getting one's back bill, or stock managed to allow one to have extra stock which can be accessed whenever needed at any time. This service not only allows one to free up space and save money but also gives one the opportunity to focus on other things.

Additionally, these services also offer free packaging reviews to ensure that your packaging meets your requirements helping you cut the costs. They also assist in the stock control and improve efficiency allowing one to get on with their business.

Overall, if you haven't thought about custom tailoring your product, it is high time you start thinking about it.

HERE'S WHY YOU SHOULD LINK BACK TO YOUR AUTHORITY SITE

Your site and blog is something that you should be proud of. The odds are you have invested your money and time to make it a great tool for serving your clients and also generate leads. However, is including external links to in your site the best idea? The links could take people away from your site or distract them from reading your content.

Don't worry, linking is a common practice expected and also respected by all kinds of users thus it is unlikely to harm your site. Below are four benefits that one could get from including external links to their sites or blogs;

1.   Makes Your Blog or Site A More Valuable and Scalable Resource

Regardless of how great your site might be, it can never contain all the relevant information or value that a user might be looking for. Therefore it makes great sense to use the power of external links to create a scalable and easy path to making your site experience better and more rewarding visits. This also not only rewards the brands you have linked but also offers your site a chance to becoming a reference resource.

2.   Search Engines Are Likely To Reward the Behavior Algorithmically

Search engines spend time analyzing spams. When doing so, they look for links with quality signals rather than spamminess. While it certainly pays considering the links you have used, links you send can be useful and usable equally. Sites with low signal quality generally link to junk substantially as compared to sites with great signal quality. These webs of trust and value can be algorithmically used by search engines to creating better search results. Use this advantage and link to resources that you know your users, as well as engines, will love.

3.   External Linking Incentivizes Links In

Sites that get links tend to do external linking to themselves. When one includes external links to their sites, then it shows that one is willing to take part in the web's linking space rather than being a closed-off individual or a purely pompous self-referential know-it-all.

4.   External Links Encourage Positive Contribution and Participation

There are lots of people on the web who are smart, talented and very dedicated that can contribute and make your efforts successful. When you include external links to your site especially in an opportunity-driven and consistent way you will be building incentives for website builders, forum participants, and other users to want to engage with your site. Incentives bring value which will essentially build your site.

There are numerous good reasons as to why including external links is suitable for your site. To maximize on your site, consider this as a tip.

HOW TO GROW YOUR INSTAGRAM FOLLOWING

Having a big Instagram following can be very lucrative for marketing and driving free traffic to your site. But there's more to it than a simple numbers game. Simply having a lot of followers doesn't necessarily mean anything. The key is having active followers – people who not only follow you but actively like and comment on your posts. These are the people that you want to target when growing your audience.

We've all heard of people buying Instagram followers, and while they have impressive numbers in the tens and hundreds of thousands, those followers don't mean anything. They are purely aesthetic in nature. That's not what we're trying to do. We want interaction with our audience.

Be Consistent

There are some simple things we can implement to help organically grow our following. The first is to post consistently. This means you want to post once a day (or every other day, or twice a day, find what fits your needs best!) and try to keep it around the same time daily. But that's not all, it also means that you should stick to a particular theme. Sure, you can absolutely post a beautiful landscape photo one day, and a picture of a gaming computer the next, but it is most beneficial to stick to one theme for all of your posts.

Interact With Your Followers

You've got the consistency down, and that's great, but it doesn't end there. You should also be interacting with the Instagram community. When someone comments on your post, take the time to acknowledge that comment – like it, and reply to them. You will notice increased interaction over time if you take the initiative of talking to your followers.

Your interaction doesn't stop at your posts. You should also spend time every day scrolling through hashtags that are relevant to the information you share on Instagram. While you scroll through it's important that you keep liking and commenting on posts. What's the best way to draw people to your page? Show genuine appreciation for their page!

Gaining Followers Quickly By Following and Unfollowing

If you are looking to quickly amass a large following there is a fairly simple and straightforward strategy you can follow that has proven itself time and time again. This requires that you find pages with large followings that are similar in content to yours. Then, in addition to following the basic rules of consistently posting within your theme, and maintaining constant interaction with your followers and the community at large, you will go to the page of your choosing and follow their followers. Typically, you want to follow between 25 and 35 in a single session. Then you should allow them some time to follow you back. If you want to increase your chances of getting a follow in return, you can like and comment on a few of their posts when you follow them. After you have allowed some time for them to follow you, you will unfollow everyone from that page that you followed before. Then simply rinse and repeat, and you will find your follower count quickly increasing with real, quality followers.

Growing your Instagram following can be very important for business purposes. If you follow the basic rules, post high-quality content, and are willing to put in the time and work, you can easily see a bump in followers almost immediately.

HOW TO ORGANIZE CONTESTS AND GIVEAWAYS TO GAIN INSTA-TRACTION

Statistics indicate that Instagram is one of the most popular social media sites in the world, clocking at least 300 million active users a day. They contribute to more than 40 billion pictures shared on the platform to date. These numbers have made Instagram the go-to site for entrepreneurs seeking to grow their business.

However, many people have gone about using Instagram all wrong, leading to sluggish traction. Some of the top Instagram personalities know the secret to gaining traction is by organizing contests and giveaways to gain insta-traction.

Contests

Contests are one of the proven ways to get insta-traction, which gives you the chance to be openly creative with your content as possible. There are different types of contests you can organize such as

Like Contests: - This involves uploading a photo and asking your fans to like it with one person or a group of individuals winning giveaways. This type of competition increases your chances of appearing on the Discover page, and it is one of the simplest ways to increase traction.

Comment Contests: - If the primary goal is to generate feedback about your products or services and increase post engagement, comment contests are the way to go. Simply upload a photo and ask your followers to comment on the post for a chance to win the prize. Always ask your followers to tag other users.

Photo Contest: - Tell users to post a photo on their personal accounts and use a hashtag of your choice – this will help you find the posts to pick a winner. To ensure insta-traction, ask your followers and fans to post pictures of them using your product and or service in creative ways.

This type of contest can also include asking your fans to repost one of your posts for a chance to win.

Giveaways

The purpose of the competition is to draw in the right followers, and the best way is to find those users is by offering giveaways that are relevant to your brand and fans. The right kinds of giveaways are those related to your brand, to bring in the right kind of insta-traction.

Simply give the rules in the caption section or provide a link to your website with a landing page that provides all the rules of getting to win the giveaway. This allows you to keep your posts short and sweet.

It all comes down to taking the word out about your contests and giveaways. Hashtags are the best way to spread the word as well as track entries. Look at the accounts of leading businesses in your niche and note the type of hashtags they are using. The right combination of hashtags will boost the exposure of your contests and giveaways, bringing in more traction.

WHY YOU SHOULD BE USING THE INSTAGRAM VIDEO FUNCTION

Instagram video content has increasingly become very popular on social media recently, and thus it is of paramount advantage for anyone looking to market him/herself to make use of this function. This shift shows that more and more business whether small or big is starting to visually communicate with their followers, customers, and fans.

The video function is one of the popularly known platforms that will enable one to leverage the power of marketing!

With more than 150 million users, Instagram is the best sharing platform. It allows one to share not only photos but also short videos. There are millions and millions of videos shared daily which is a great reason why one should utilize this platform. Below are some of the main advantages of using this function;

Increased Engagement

Unlike video posts on Twitter or Facebook that are sometimes overlooked by users regardless of their quality, Instagram videos are rarely missed. According to a study done by Forrester, Instagram videos generate more engagement 58 times than Facebook and 120 times than Twitter. Having an Instagram account with interesting and useful content can earn one with crazy levels of engagement with the audience.

Building Personality and Trust

Since more content is becoming popular, one of the key benefits of using the video function is that it helps one build trust. People buy from people they can trust, and Instagram video feature will help you create that emotional connection with your audience. The significant thing here is that this function allows one to share their day-to-day experience in a casual and informal way giving followers, fans, and customers a feel for one's business.

Sharing behind the scene activities has been noted to rank well on Instagram, particularly if it is a service provider. Such videos make one's company more trustworthy and attractive which in turn positively affects one's marketing.

Increase in Traffic

Even though one cannot add clickable links to the videos, they still are a dominant source of traffic. Moreover with the levels of engagement being higher than Twitter and Facebook, using the video function can be tremendously useful for your site's visibility.

Gaining a Competitive Edge

Competition on Instagram is still far less than in Twitter or Facebook. The American Express Survey reported that nearly 2% of small business are currently embracing the Instagram video function and they have gained an advantage over their competitors. Thus is clear that by using the video function, one is likely to reach their target audience faster and easier.

Free Advertising

Yes, that is correct. The great thing about using Instagram video function is free publicity. One can showcase their services and products in action generating large exposure. The feature gives one an opportunity to show off what they are offering.

Embrace the video function and be rewarded!

www.ingramcontent.com/pod-product-compliance
Lightning Source LLC
Chambersburg PA
CBHW071115220526
45467CB00004B/1894